Biblical Financial Study

Collegiate Edition

Teacher's Guide

Crown Ministries

Longwood, Florida 32750-6758

September 1998 Edition

TABLE OF CONTENTS

INTRODUCTION TO TEACHER'S GUIDE

THE CROWN MINISTRIES BIBLICAL FINANCIAL STUDY

The *Collegiate Edition* of the Crown Ministries Financial Study is designed to be taught in either a classroom or small group setting.

 CLASSROOM (This icon identifies information for those teaching in a *classroom* setting.)

 SMALL GROUP (This icon is applicable to those leading the study in a *small group* setting.)

THE TEACHER'S GUIDE

The Teacher's Guide is divided into five sections:

1. **Information every teacher and leader needs to know**

2. **Information classroom teachers need to know**

3. **Information small group leaders need to know**

4. **Weekly homework guides**

5. **Small group leaders — student evaluations, care logs and prayer logs**

   There are two sets of the student evaluations, care logs and prayer logs so the leaders can use one set for their first group and photocopy the blank set for subsequent groups that they lead.

CROWN'S WEB SITE

Encourage your students to regularly visit Crown's web site **www.crown.org** and click on "Students". They will find many helpful resources – from a categorized list of the verses dealing with money and possessions to more detailed information about subjects such as budgeting, insurance and mutual funds. There are also links to many other informative web sites.

INORMATION EVERY TEACHER AND LEADER NEEDS TO KNOW

OBJECTIVES OF THE STUDY

1. **Encourage students to experience more intimate fellowship with Christ.**

Luke 16:11 expresses the correlation between how we handle our resources and the quality of our fellowship with the Lord: *"If therefore you have not been faithful in the use of worldly wealth, who will entrust the true riches to you?"*

2. **Challenge students to invite Jesus Christ to be their Lord.**

Money is a primary competitor with Christ for the lordship of our lives. Matthew 6:24 reads, *"No man can serve two masters, you will love one and hate the other . . . you cannot serve God and Mammon* (money)*."*

3. **Help students put their financial house in order.**

4. **Build close relationships among the participants.**

TEACHER TRAINING REQUIREMENTS

Every teacher needs to participate in leader training. Those who have led a Crown Ministries adult Small Group Study will be qualified to teach the collegiate study in a classroom or in a small group.

Contact Crown Ministries for details on leader training.

TEACHER'S AUDIO TAPE

HOW TO LEAD AUDIO TAPE

Every teacher must listen to Side One of the tape titled *How to Lead a Crown Ministries Collegiate Study* before leading the study.

 Side Two is titled *What the Small Group Leader Needs to Know Each Week.* Each week the small group leader should listen to the portion of Side Two covering the lesson they are preparing to lead.

Crown Ministries has studies for four other age categories:

The ABC's of Handling Money God's Way, which is for children age 7 and younger.

This book is full of activities to help make learning basic financial principles fun and exciting. It is designed to be very "hands-on" because children learn from doing. The *ABC's Leader's Guide* offers the teacher a wide variety of optional activities that reinforce the financial concepts in ways that appeal to young children. This hard-bound study is published in full color. **It is never too early to start training children!**

The Secret, for ages 8 to 12.

Four children with a financial challenge learn the secret of giving, saving, spending and much more. They also discover that they can trust God to provide. **The principles are imbedded in a story of adventure that captures and holds the attention of children.** The study is in a beautifully bound, hard-cover book with color illustrations, **and makes learning about money fun!**

Teens

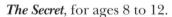

Teens love this study! Besides memorizing a key scripture and learning what God says about money, there is also a practical financial exercise at the end of each chapter designed to help teens create habits that **will set them on a life-long journey of handling money responsibly**.

Small group study for adults

This remarkably effective small group study changes lives! It is thoroughly biblical and very practical!

HOW TO PLACE AN ORDER

Orders should be placed at least three weeks prior to time needed!

The *Collegiate Financial Study* may be ordered by telephoning (407) 331-6000, over the Internet at Crown's web site www.crown.org or by mail. If you order by mail:

1. **Complete the order form.** Photocopy and complete the order form on the next page. Be sure to *use a street address* as Crown normally ships materials UPS.
2. **Pay for the order.** Please enclose a check with the order.
3. **Where to send the order and check:** Crown Ministries, 530 Crown Oak Centre Drive, Longwood, Florida 32750.

 Academic institutions have their own procedures and timing for ordering course materials. Please provide these instructions to the person responsible for ordering materials for this class.

MORE ABOUT CROWN MINISTRIES

MISSION STATEMENT

Training people to be financially faithful in order to know Christ more intimately and to be free to serve Him.

WHAT IS CROWN MINISTRIES?

Crown Ministries is an interdenominational ministry that trains people, primarily in small groups, to apply the financial principles from the Bible to their lives.

FINANCIAL INFORMATION

Crown Ministries is a non-profit, tax-exempt organization. It is governed by a Board of Directors, none of whom receive a salary from serving the ministry. Book royalties are the property of the ministry. Crown is a member of the Evangelical Council for Financial Accountability, whose members must adhere to certain standards, including an annual audit. It is funded by course tuition and by donations, the bulk of which come from those who have taken the study or churches that are implementing Crown.

PROMOTING FINANCIAL PRODUCTS OR SERVICES

No one may use their affiliation with Crown Ministries to promote or influence the sale of any investments or financial services or professional services.

Order Form

Date: _____

Mr. ❑   Mrs. ❑   Miss ❑

| | | | | | | | | | | | | | | | | | | | | | | | | | | | | | | | | | | | | | | | |

Street Address:

| | | | | | | | | | | | | | | | | | | | | | | | | | | | | | | | | | | | | | | | |

City: State: Zip:

| | | | | | | | | | | | | | | | | | | | | | | | | | | — | | | |

Home Phone: Work Phone:

| | | — | | | — | | | | | | | — | | | — | | | |

E-Mail Address:

| | | | | | | | | | | | | | | | | | | | | | | | | | | | | | | | | | | | | | | | |

Item	Price	Quantity	Total
The ABC's of Handling Money God's Way (Ages 7 and younger)	$12.00		
The ABC's Teacher's Guide	$10.00		
The Secret (Ages 8 to 12)	$20.00		
The Secret Leader's Guide	$10.00		
Crown Financial Study for Teens	$15.00		
Teen Leader's Guide	$10.00		
How to Lead Teen's and Children's Studies Audio Tape	$ 6.00		
Collegiate Financial Study	$25.00		
Collegiate Teacher's Guide	$10.00		
		TOTAL	

Please enclose a check made payable to: **Crown Ministries, Inc., 530 Crown Oak Centre Drive, Longwood, FL, 32750-6758.** Orders may also be placed by phone at (407) 331-6000 or by visiting Crown's web site at www.crown.org

Shipping and handling ($3.50 for orders less than $35.00; over $35.00, add 10% of order total):

Please add applicable state and local sales tax for AL, AR, AZ, CA, Fl, GA, IN, KS, MI, MS, NC, NV, VA, WA

ORDER TOTAL

Prices subject to change

COURSE DESCRIPTION

This course may be offered as a one or two credit hour course. It requires a minimum of ten sessions to complete. Daily homework, Bible study, practical exercises and weekly memorization of Scripture are required. Since typical semesters are 14 weeks, there is adequate time for examinations and the teaching of additional subjects. Written papers and book reviews are optional.

COURSE OBJECTIVES

The objectives of this course are:

1. **To teach the practical financial principles of Scripture.**

    Topics include work, spending, saving, debt, giving and many other important financial issues students will need to know after graduation.

2. **To encourage students to experience more intimate fellowship with Christ.**

    Luke 16:11 expresses the correlation between how we handle money and the quality of our fellowship with the Lord: *"If therefore you have not been faithful in the use of worldly wealth, who will entrust the true riches to you?"*

3. **To challenge students to invite Jesus Christ to be their Lord.**

    Money is a primary competitor with Christ for the lordship of our lives. Matthew 6:24 reads, *"No one can serve two masters. You will love one and hate the other ... you cannot serve God and Mammon (money)."* As students learn God's perspective on possessions and His intended use of money, they are challenged to submit to the Lord and other areas of their life.

SAMPLES

The following are offered to teachers as samples which can be modified as they see fit. They are included for the convenience of the teachers.

1. Course Syllabus

2. Bibliography

3. Sample Papers

4. Midterm and Final Examinations

SAMPLE COURSE SYLLABUS (may be adapted to one or two hour course)

Week	Sample Schedule	Week	Sample Schedule
1	General Introduction	8	Honesty / Chapter 6
2	Introduction / Chapter 1	9	Counsel / Chapter 7
3	God's Part / Chapter 2	10	Giving / Chapter 8
4	Our Part / Chapter 3	11	Lecture on subject selected by teacher
5	Work / Chapter 4	12	Investing / Chapter 9
6	Debt / Chapter 5	13	Your Future / Chapter 10
7	Midterm exam or lecture on by subject selected by teacher	14	Final exam or lecture on subject selected by teacher

ADDITIONAL STUDY

To further enhance the students' ability to manage their personal finances and to meet potential academic requirements, we recommend the teacher consider using *Personal Finance*, 5th edition, by Kapoor, Dlabay and Hughes (Irwin McGraw-Hill). Below we have noted the appropriate chapters that correspond to the ten chapters in the *Collegiate Edition* of the Crown Ministries study. Other personal finance textbooks may also be suitable for this additional study.

Crown Chapter:	*Personal Finance* Reference:
1	None
2	Part I, Chapter 1: Personal Financial Planning
3	Part I, Chapter 2: Financial Aspects of Career Planning
4	Part I, Chapter 2: Appendix: Resumés, Cover Letters and Interviews
5	Part II, Chapter 5: The Banking Services of Financial Institutions Part II, Chapter 6: Introduction to Consumer Credit
6	Part I, Chapter 3: Money Management Strategy; Financial Statements and Budgeting
7	Part II, Chapter 7: Choosing a Source of Credit; The Cost of Credit Alternatives
8	Part III, Chapter 8: Consumer Purchasing Strategies and Legal Protection
9	Part IV, Chapters 10,11,12: Home and Automobile Insurance; Health and Disability Insurance; Life Insurance Part V, Chapters 13, 14, 15, 16, 17: Fundamentals of Investing; Investing in Stocks; Investing in Bonds; Investing in Mutual Funds; Real Estate and Other Investment Alternatives
10	Part VI, Chapters 18,19: Retirement Planning; Estate Planning Part I, Chapter 4: Planning Your Tax Strategy Part III, Chapter 9: The Finances of Housing

SAMPLE BIBLIOGRAPHY

The following are suggested books for the students for future study or assignments. Have the students write a report on each book selected.

A Life Well Spent, Russ Crosson, Word Publishers

Margin, Dr. Richard Swenson, NAV Press

Master Your Money, Ron Blue, Nelson Publishers

The Millionaire Next Door, Thomas J. Stanley, Ph,D., and William D. Danko, Ph.D. Pocket Books

Money, Possessions and Eternity, Randy Alcorn, Tyndale House Publishers

The Wall Street Journal Guide to Understanding Money and Investing, Kenneth M. Marks and A. Siegel, Fireside

What Color is Your Parachute?, Richard Nelson Bolles, Ten Speed Press

Your Money Counts, Howard Dayton, Tyndale House Publishers

SAMPLE PAPERS

Subject	
Work	*My Life in Five Years* — This paper is designed to help students think through the transition from college to career and should encompass their profession and lifestyle (home, car, activities and family).
Debt	Do research into debt in this country by choosing one of the following topics: *Personal Debt in America; Credit Card Debt and Delinquency; College Loans and Delinquencies; Consumer Debt; Automobile Loans; Bankruptcy in America.*
Honesty	*The Economic Consequences of Dishonesty in the Workplace* or *Deceptiveness in Advertising*
Giving	*The Role Christians Should Take in Serving the Poor in Our Nation and the World*
Giving	Have the students volunteer several hours working in an organization that serves the poor. Write a paper on this experience and God's view of the poor.
Investing	Research various checking accounts at local banks and stock brokerage companies. What are the fees, minimum balances and other restrictions? What is the cost of using the ATM machines at this bank and at other locations? What interest does the bank pay on interest bearing accounts? Write a paper on why you would select one over the other.
Investing	Using an 800 number (from the business section of the newspaper) call one or two mutual funds and request information on the funds. Write a paper on why you would select one fund over another.
Gambling	Research the impact gambling is having on our society.
Cumulative	Describe your view of biblical stewardship. (Do not limit this to the area of giving.)
Cumulative	Contrast our culture's perspective and use of money with a biblical view.
Cumulative	Develop a plan and rationale to become financially free within a specified period of time.

MIDTERM EXAM

MIDTERM EXAM — SAMPLE QUESTIONS

1. Write two of the six Scripture memory passages in their entirety, including biblical references.

2. Discuss the differences between God's economy and the way most people handle their money. (essay)

3. Circle the name that best describes God's part in the area of money:

    (a) Almighty

    (b) Master

    (c) King

    (d) Steward

4. List three reasons why God allows difficult circumstances.

5. What word best describes our part in the area of money?

6. What does the Bible say about hard work and laziness?

7. What is the biblical view of rest?

8. Daniel modeled six characteristics of a godly employee. Name at least three. (Daniel 6:1-21 may help.)

9. Contrast retirement as it is practiced in our culture with what the Scriptures teach.

10. Which of the following describes what our major financial responsibility is to be?

    (a) Servant

    (b) Faithful

    (c) Responsible

    (d) Trusting

11. Define debt. Describe how it was viewed in the Old Testament and the cause of a person getting into debt.

12. Define cosigning and describe God's perspective of cosigning.

13. Explain why credit card companies want you to become a borrower.

14. Write a short essay on two of the following:

    (a) How will understanding God's part with money impact my life?

    (b) Describe how learning about God's ownership of your possessions and His control of circumstances will help you learn to be content.

    (c) Describe the contrast between our culture's view of work and a biblical perspective of work.

FINAL EXAM

FINAL EXAM — SAMPLE QUESTIONS

1. Write three Scripture memory passages in their entirety, including biblical references.
2. Describe God's attitude in giving and what our attitude should be.
3. List three ways a person is blessed by giving.
4. Define the tithe.
5. Why does the Lord bless us financially when we give? What does He expect of us?
6. Define counsel and name at least three types of people who should be considered as counselors.
7. How is the Bible a source of counsel?
8. Who should not be among our counselors and why not?
9. When should a non-Christian be a counselor?
10. Why is it particularly important for leaders to be absolutely honest?
11. Define a bribe and describe the biblical position on bribes.
12. Define restitution. How should we apply the principle of restitution?
13. Describe the steps in setting up a budget
14. Define a procrastinator. Is procrastination biblical?
15. What does the Bible say about saving? Give an example from Scripture.
16. Circle the three elements of compound interest:
    (a) Time
    (b) The Bank
    (c) Amount
    (d) The Stock Market
    (e) Interest Rate
17. What is the biblical view of gambling?
18. Why should adults have a will?
19. What does the Bible say about paying taxes?
20. Who is responsible to train children how to handle money properly?
21. Define coveting and greed. What does the Bible say about coveting and greed? How does our culture promote coveting and greed?
22. What does God say about contentment? How can a person learn to be content? How does our culture discourage contentment?
23. According to the Bible, what are the dangers of wealth?
24. Why should godly people not worry or become envious of the wicked who become prosperous?
25. List three reasons why godly people may not prosper.
26. What are the four steps outlined in Matthew 18:15-17 for resolving a dispute with a fellow Christian?
27. What does Scripture say about showing favoritism? Is favoritism just showing partiality to the wealthy?
28. Write an essay on one of the following subjects:
    (a) The difference between the poverty, steward and prosperity mindset.
    (b) The major areas of our responsibility as a faithful steward.
    (c) What hinders people from seeking counsel?

SMALL GROUP LEADER RESPONSIBILITIES

1. Unconditionally love and encourage your students.

People are more receptive to spiritual truth when they have been loved. People want to know how much you care before they care how much you know.

2. Hold your students accountable.

Small Group Leaders must insure that students memorize the assigned Scriptures and have prepared the homework and practical application. If a student has failed to do this, do not allow him or her to participate in answering the homework questions.

3. Model faithfulness.

Luke 6:40 reads, *"Everyone, after he has been fully trained, will be like his teacher."* The teacher must be faithful in every area. Always arrive early, pray consistently for your students, know your memory verses fluently, and have your homework and practical applications prepared.

THE SMALL GROUP STUDY

SIZE OF THE SMALL GROUP STUDY

There should be no more than **eight** students and there should be **two** leaders in each group.

SMALL GROUP MEETINGS

The groups meet for two hours once each week for ten weeks. The time and day the group meets should be the one most convenient to the participants. Groups may meet anywhere — in homes, dorms or churches.

STUDENT EVALUATION SHEET

The Student Evaluation Sheets are found on pages 75 and 87 and should be used by the small group leader to record the performance of the students after each class.

As the small group is being assembled, the leaders should diligently **pray** that the Lord will bring just the right students into the group. Then the leaders should meet with their students as a group at least **one week** before the study begins for the following reasons:

1. **Start to love the students and build relationships.**

2. **Review the students' requirements.**

   The requirements are designed to take approximately two hours outside of class each week and, if for any reason someone comes to the class unprepared, they will not be allowed to participate in the discussion. The student requirements are:

   ❑ Daily homework

   ❑ Scripture to memorize each week

   ❑ Weekly practical application

   ❑ Daily prayer for each participant

   ❑ Attend at least eight of the ten classes

3. **Describe the other important "ground rules".**

   ❑ The class opens and closes in prayer.

   ❑ Scriptures are memorized in the version used in the Crown Ministries materials and not in another version of the Bible.

   ❑ The classes start and stop precisely on time.

   ❑ Group discussions are strictly confidential.

   ❑ Students will be trained to be leaders by each person leading one week.

   ❑ No one will be embarrassed by being required to expose their financial situation.

4. **Dispense and collect payment for the materials.**

   One student set is required for each person.

5. **Assign the Week 1 homework.**

   The assignment is found on page 5 of the Student Manual and must be completed prior to attending Week 1. The assignment is to memorize *Luke 16:11* and answer the homework questions.

   Ask the students to bring their calendar to the first class to schedule the two socials (see page 22).

To help the students develop a more consistent prayer life, we utilize the prayer log.

❏ During the first class, have each person tell the others the information asked for at the top of the prayer log — their name, phone number, address and e-mail address. One prayer log should be filled out for each person. The prayer logs are located in the back of the Student Manual and the Teacher's Guide.

❏ End each class by taking prayer requests from each member. The requests need not be limited to financial concerns. Prior to taking a request inquire if they have experienced any answers to their prayer requests. There may be more than one request per week.

❏ **Ask the participants to complete their own prayer log before coming to class to save time.** Each member is required to pray daily for every member in the small group during the ten weeks. *Examine the sample prayer log below.*

P R A Y E R   L O G

Name: Ernie A. Degree

Phone: 555-1234

Address: Room 317, Jackson Hall, Raleigh, N.C. 72212

E-mail Address:

Week	Prayer Request(s)	Answers To Prayer
1	Broken relationship in my family	
2	Need job to help with finances	Relationship mending
3	Need job	
4	Need to improve relationship with roommate	Got good job
5	Summer employment and plans	

1. **Open with prayer.**

2. **Individually recite the Scripture to memorize.**

3. **Confirm that the Practical Applications and Homework have been completed.**

4. **Conduct the group discussion.** The discussion should proceed as follows:

    ❑ Different group members read the Scriptures for a particular day's homework.

    ❑ Proceed in a circle asking every person to answer **all** the questions for that day's home-work. If it becomes apparent you will have difficulty ending on time, ask the students to abbreviate their answers or limit the number of students who share their answers.

5 . **Complete the items listed in the Remaining Agenda.**

6. **Play the Practical Application video.**

7. **Share prayer requests and write them in the Prayer Logs.**

8. **End in prayer.**

NOTE: Small Group Dynamics

The most effective group discussions involve group interaction and mem-ber-to-member participation.

❑ In diagram 1 the sole focus is on the small group leader who does all the talking. The students are passive. This is **not** how Crown Ministries is designed.

❑ Diagram 2 reflects a group interacting with one another and a leader who guides and facilitates the discussion. The leader must establish an environment in which students have the freedom to express their in-sights and questions.

Leader

Diagram 1 — The Wrong Method

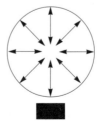

Leader

Diagram 2 — The Correct Method

1. **Love the students outside of class.**

    ❏ **Care log**

        • The purpose of the Care Log is to insure that the small group leaders contact their students each week to encourage and love them. (The Care Logs are on pages 78 and 90.)

        • The weekly contacts may be by telephone, mail, e-mail or in person.

        • The two leaders should alternate each week in their responsibility to contact the students by deciding who will contact students on the odd numbered weeks and who will contact the students on the even numbered weeks.

        • The students should not be aware of the Care Log.

        • The leaders should inspect each other's Care Log weekly to encourage faithfulness.

CARE LOG

Leaders: _John Cole and Tim Manor_

Beginning Date of Small Group Study: _January 5_

Initials of Leader responsible for contact	STUDENTS	T. Turner	B. Hunt	J. Morgan	G. Jones		
WEEK 1	JC	called 1/13	lunch	called 1/14	postcard 1/13		
2	TM	called 1/20	called 1/21	wrote 1/13	saw in person		
3	JC						
4	TM						

DESCRIPTION OF FIRST SOCIAL ACTIVITY (Week Five): _Pizza dinner at John Cole's home_

DESCRIPTION OF SECOND SOCIAL ACTIVITY (Week Ten): _Coffee at Java Shop_

❏ **Socials**

- The small group leaders should organize two social events for the students. These activities may be for dessert, pizza or any other relaxed setting that will encourage the development of relationships. The socials may be held before or after class.

- The first social should be scheduled mid-way through the study.

- The second social should be held as soon as possible after the study.

❏ **Visit the students where they work, attend school or live.**

2. **Love the students inside of class.**

❏ The leader's attitude should be loving, humble and caring — not a critical or a "know-it-all" attitude. We are students-among-students, in that we all are growing in understanding the unfathomable Word of God.

❏ As students answer questions, encourage, affirm and thank them.

❏ If an answer is incorrect, be careful not to discourage the student by responding harshly or negatively.

❏ Maintain good eye contact and be attentive. We communicate through our body language.

CROWN'S OVERVIEW OF CHAPTER 1

The primary objectives for Chapter 1 are to begin to develop close relationships among the participants and reinforce the study requirements.

Note: The blank space following each agenda number is for the small group teacher to fill in the scheduled time for each agenda item. For example, if your class begins at 7:00, # 1 would read 7:00, # 2 would read 7:05, # 3 would read 7:10, # 4 would read 8:20 and so forth. This is designed to assist the teacher in monitoring the time so that the class will end punctually.

Agenda:

1. _____(5 minutes) Open in prayer.

2. _____(5 minutes) Have each person individually recite from memory Luke 16:11. If any student has not memorized Luke 16:11 or completed the homework assignment, they may not participate in the homework discussion, # 4 below.

> *"If therefore you have not been faithful in the use of worldly wealth*, who will entrust the true riches to you?"* (Luke 16:11).

3. _____(70 minutes) Have each person introduce themselves, beginning with a leader. Ask them to share how they were introduced to Jesus Christ and something of their family background. To determine how much time each person is allotted, divide the number of people into 70 minutes. The leaders should communicate this time constraint. If a student is too brief, the leader should gently ask additional questions to provide an opportunity for him to express himself more fully.

4. _____(10 minutes) Begin the homework discussion.

Note: Crown's comments, in brackets, will follow each question. Following Crown's comments there will be a space for the teacher's answer.

Read Isaiah 55:8-9.

Based on this passage, do you think God's financial principles differ from the way most people handle money?

[God's financial principles contrast sharply with the way most people handle money.]

What do you think would be the greatest difference?

[Most people do not believe the Lord plays a role in finances, but Scripture reveals He has the dominant role.]

Then read Luke 16:11.

What does this verse communicate to you about the importance of managing possessions faithfully?

[How we handle money has a direct impact on our fellowship with Christ.]

How does handling money impact our fellowship with the Lord?

[If we are unfaithful with money, our fellowship with the Lord will suffer.]

REMAINING AGENDA _____ (10 minutes)

- Complete the God's Part Homework on pages 11 to 15 in the student manual. Do the homework daily.
- Memorize *1 Chronicles 29:11-12* (remind the students to begin immediately because of the length of this passage).
- Complete the practical applications of Recording Income and Spending and of the Personal Financial Statement.

 If you are leading the study in a small group, you should also: _____ (20 minutes)

1. Review the calendar to determine if any regularly scheduled classes fall on a holiday. If there are any conflicts, please reschedule at this meeting.
2. Schedule the two socials.
3. Complete the Prayer Logs. Each participant should have one Prayer Log for each person or couple, including himself.
4. Take prayer requests and note them in the Prayer Log.
5. End in prayer.

 Reminder for Small Group Leaders: Complete the students' evaluations. Be sure to contact each student this week.

CROWN OVERVIEW OF CHAPTER 2

In many respects this is the most important section because the remainder of the study will build upon understanding God's Part. The Lord's ownership of all things is foundational.

Agenda:

1. _____(5 minutes) Open in prayer.

2. _____(5 minutes) Have each person individually recite from memory:

> *"Everything in the heavens and earth is yours, O Lord, and this is your kingdom. We adore you as being in control of everything. Riches and honor come from you alone, and you are the Ruler of all mankind; your hand controls power and might, and it is at your discretion that men are made great and given strength"* (1 Chronicles 29:11-12,LB).

3. _____(5 minutes) Confirm that everyone has completed the practical application of Personal Financial Statement and has started keeping a record of all spending.

4. _____(80 minutes) Begin the small group discussion.

Reminder for small group leader: The discussion for each day's homework should proceed as follows: (1) Read the Scriptures. Assign one passage of Scripture from that day's homework to each person to read (as far as the verses will go); (2) Proceed in a circle, asking each person to answer all the questions for that day's homework. For example: "Bob, how did you answer the questions for day three?" If you are running out of time, ask the students to be brief in their responses.

DAY ONE_____

Read Deuteronomy 10:14; Psalm 24:1 and 1 Corinthians 10:26. What do these passages teach about the ownership of your possessions?

[The Lord owns everything in the world.]

Then read Leviticus 25:23; Psalm 50:10-12 and Haggai 2:8. List the specific items in these verses that the Lord owns?

Leviticus 25:23 — [God owns all the land.]

Psalm 50:10-12 — [God owns all the animals.]

Haggai 2:8 — [God owns all the gold and silver.]

Prayerfully evaluate your attitude of ownership toward your possessions. Do you consistently recognize the true owner of those possessions?

Give two practical suggestions to help recognize God's ownership.

1.

2.

DAY TWO_____

Read 1 Chronicles 29:11-12 and Psalm 135:6. What do these verses say about the Lord's control of circumstances?

[The Lord is in control of all circumstances.]

Then read Proverbs 21:1; Isaiah 40:21-24 and Acts 17:26. What do these passages tell you about the Lord's control of people?

Proverbs 21:1 — [God controls the heart of each person.]

Isaiah 40:21-24 — [The Lord is in absolute control of all humankind.]

Acts 17:26 — [The Lord controls the boundaries and duration of every nation.]

Do you normally recognize the Lord's control of all events? If not, how can you become more consistent in recognizing His control?

DAY THREE

Read Genesis 45:4-8; Genesis 50:19-20 and Romans 8:28. Why is it important to realize that God controls and uses even difficult circumstances for good in the life of a godly person?

[God works every circumstance for good in the lives of those who love Him and are yielded to His Lordship. Joseph suffered difficult circumstances, but God orchestrated those difficulties for ultimate good.]

How does this perspective impact you today?

Share a difficult circumstance you have experienced and how the Lord ultimately used it for good in your life.

 Small Group Leader, you should have approximately **one hour** *of class time remaining. We recommend a three-minute stretch break for your group at this time.*

DAY FOUR

Read Psalm 34:9-10; Matthew 6:31-33 and Philippians 4:19. What has the Lord promised concerning meeting your needs?

[God has promised to provide our needs if we seek first His kingdom and righteousness.]

Give a biblical example of the Lord providing for needs in a supernatural way.

[Israel in the wilderness, Jesus feeding five thousand, and the Lord sending ravens to feed Elijah.]

How does this apply to you today?

DAY FIVE

Read the God's Part Notes. Describe the most important concept in God's Part.

How can you work to be consistent in recognizing the Lord's ownership of your possessions?

[Encourage the students to meditate on 1 Chronicles 29:11-12 for the next thirty days.]

What personal benefits do you anticipate from this consistency?

DAY SIX

What three goals do you want to accomplish during the next five to ten years?

Describe what financial resources will be required to accomplish your goals. What is your plan to acquire the necessary finances?

As you think of yourself as an older person, what do you wish to be remembered for?

In view of your answers to these questions what action do you need to take?

REMAINING AGENDA _____(10 minutes)

Review what the students are required to do for the next lesson:

- Complete the Our Part Homework on pages 25 to 29 in the Student Manual.
- Memorize *1 Corinthians 4:2.*
- Complete the practical applications of Deed and Career and Financial Goals.

For small groups, in addition to the Remaining Agenda above: _____(15 minutes)

1. Note in the Prayer Log requests and answers to prayers.
2. End in prayer.

Reminder for Small Group Leaders: Remember to be open and vulnerable with your own struggles in this area. Contact each student this week and record the communication in the Care Log.

CROWN'S OVERVIEW OF CHAPTER 3

We have the responsibility to be faithful stewards of the possessions God entrusts to us, and the Lord will hold us accountable for how we handle them.

Agenda:

1. _____(5 minutes) Open in prayer.

2. _____(5 minutes) Have each person individually recite from memory:

> *"Moreover, it is required in stewards that a man be found faithful"* (1 Corinthians 4:2, KJV).

3. _____(5 minutes) Confirm that everyone has completed the Deed and Career and Financial Goals practical applications. Have two people witness each Deed.

4. _____(80 minutes) Begin the small group discussion.

DAY ONE

Read Genesis 1:26 and Psalm 8:4-6. What do these verses say about the authority God gave people?

[People were given authority over the Lord's possessions.]

Then read 1 Corinthians 4:2. According to this verse what is your requirement as a steward?

[We are required to be *faithful* as stewards.]

How would you define a steward?

[A steward is a manager or trustee of another's property.]

DAY TWO

Read the parable of the talents in Matthew 25:14-30. What does the parable illustrate about the following:

1. Our authority as stewards *(Matthew 25:14)?*

[The Lord gives us authority as stewards over His property.]

2. Our responsibilities?

[We are to be faithful with whatever the Lord gives us, and we are expected to act and not be lazy because of fear.]

3. Our being held accountable for our actions *(Matthew 25:19)*?

[We are going to be held accountable for how we manage possessions (we will also be held accountable for how we use our time and talents). This parable does not teach that a believer can lose his or her salvation if unfaithful in handling possessions.]

4. What blessings did the master give to the faithful stewards *(Matthew 25:20-23)*?

[They were given greater responsibilities and the opportunity of entering into the joy of the master.]

5. What other principles are applicable to you?

DAY THREE

Read Luke 16:1-2. Why did the master remove the steward from his position?

[The steward was removed because he squandered the master's possessions.]

Have you observed the Lord removing people from positions of authority because they were unfaithful? If so, describe the circumstances.

How do you think this principle is applicable to you today?

 *Small Group Leader, you should have approximately **one hour** of class time remaining. We recommend a three-minute stretch break for your group at this time.*

DAY FOUR

Read Luke 16:10. Describe the principle found in this verse.

[If a person is unfaithful in a little matter, he or she will be unfaithful in much. And if a person is faithful in little, he will be faithful in much.]

How does this apply in your situation?

Then read Luke 16:12. Are we required to be faithful with other people's possessions? What happens if we are not?

[Yes. If one is unfaithful with that which is another's, the Lord will not entrust him with possessions of his own.]

How does this apply to you?

DAY FIVE

Read the Our Part Notes. How have you observed the Lord using money to mold your character?

What strengths have been developed in your character?

What weaknesses in your character still need to be addressed?

DAY SIX

PONDER YOUR FUTURE

Read Psalm 90:10,12 and Isaiah 40:6-7. If you remain healthy, how long can you expect to live?

[We can expect to live 70 to 80 years.]

Why do you think the Lord in *Psalm 90:10,12* encourages us to number the days we think we will live on earth?

[Numbering our days reminds us how brief life really is, and helps motivate us to invest our time in eternally significant things.]

Read Romans 14:10-12; 1 Corinthians 3:12-15 and 2 Corinthians 5:9-10. What will happen to each of us in the future?

Romans 14:10-12 — [We will stand before the judgment seat of God and give an account of our actions.]

1 Corinthians 3:12 - 15 — [All our actions will be tested by the Lord, and we will be rewarded only for those which are pleasing to Him.]

2 Corinthians 5:9-10 — [Our ambition should be to please the Lord, for we will be required to account for every action.]

In your own words contrast the length of your life with eternity.

How will this impact the way you live and spend money?

REMAINING AGENDA _____ (10 minutes)

Review what the students are required to do for the next lesson.
- Complete the Work Homework on pages 39 to 44 in the Student Manual.
- Memorize *Colossians 3:23-24* .
- Complete the practical applications of Resumé and Job Interview.

 For small groups, in addition to the Remaining Agenda items above: _____ (15 minutes)

1. Note on the Prayer Log requests and answers to prayers. Encourage everyone to be faithful to pray for each other daily.
2. End in prayer.

 Reminder for Small Group Leaders: This week, at the latest, schedule a social event for the group. Also, pray for everyone in your group each day. This is your most important task.

CROWN'S OVERVIEW OF CHAPTER 4

Work can be one of the most fulfilling or frustrating areas of life. Our satisfaction is dependent upon our understanding the Lord's perspective of work.

Agenda:

1. _____ (5 minutes) Open in prayer.

2. _____ (5 minutes) Have everyone individually recite from memory:

> *"Whatever you do, do your work heartily, as for the Lord rather than for men; knowing that from the Lord you will receive the reward of the inheritance. It is the Lord Christ whom you serve"* (Colossians 3:23-24).

3. _____ (5 minutes) Confirm that everyone has completed the Resumé and Job Interview practical application.

4. _____ (80 minutes) Begin the small group discussion.

DAY ONE

Read Genesis 2:15. Did the Lord institute work prior to sin entering the world? Why is this important to recognize?

[Yes, work was instituted prior to sin entering the world. In the perfect, sinless environment of the Garden of Eden, God created work for man's benefit — work is not a result of sin and the curse.]

Then read Genesis 3:17-19. What was the consequence of sin on work?

[Work became difficult as a result of sin.]

Then read Exodus 20:9 and 2 Thessalonians 3:10-12. What do these passages communicate to you about work?

Exodus 20:9 — [Old Testament believers were required to work six days each week.]

2 Thessalonians 3:10-12 — [In the New Testament work is also required. This verse does not recommend hunger for those who cannot work because of physical or mental limitations; only those who are capable of working but choose not to work.]

DAY TWO_____

Read Genesis 39:2-5; Exodus 35:30-35; Exodus 36:1-2 and Psalm 75:6-7. What do each of these verses tell us about the Lord's involvement in our work?

Genesis 39:2-5 — [The Lord is in control of success.]

Exodus 35:30-35 — [The Lord gives us job skills and the ability to teach.]

Exodus 36:1-2 — [The Lord gives us our skills and understanding.]

Psalm 75:6-7 — [The Lord controls promotion and demotion.]

How do these truths differ from the way people view work at the job or at school?

[The biblical perspective of God's part in work is in remarkable contradiction to the culture around us that does not acknowledge the Lord in work.]

How will this perspective impact your work?

[Our work attitudes and actions should be dramatically different from those who do not recognize God's role in work. We should be humble in our accomplishments because God gives us skills, success and promotion.]

DAY THREE_____

Read Ephesians 6:5-9; Colossians 3:22-25 and 1 Peter 2:18. What responsibilities does the employee have according to these verses?

[Sincere obedience to employer — even one who is not good and gentle; work as unto the Lord; work heartily.]

For whom do you really work? How will this understanding alter your work performance?

[We work for the Lord. Having this perspective will allow us to make a sincere effort — even in difficult circumstances — to serve those who are our superiors or subordinates.]

 *Small Group Leader, you should have approximately **one hour** of class time remaining. We recommend a three-minute stretch break for your group at this time.*

DAY FOUR

Read Proverbs 6:6-11; Proverbs 18:9 and 2 Thessalonians 3:7-9. What is God's perspective on working hard?

Proverbs 6:6-11 — [Ants are commended for saving.]

Proverbs 18:9 — [Laziness is condemned.]

2 Thessalonians 3:7-9 — [Paul was a model of hard work.]

Do you work hard? If not, describe what steps you will take to improve your work habits.

Then read Exodus 34:21. What does this verse communicate to you about rest?

[Hard work should be balanced with adequate rest and tempered by other biblical priorities — even during busy times, one day of each week was required.]

Do you get sufficient rest?

How do you guard against overwork?

DAY FIVE

Read the Work Notes and answer: What in the notes proved especially interesting or challenging?

How will this impact you?

Do you usually recognize that you are working for the Lord? If not, what will you do to improve this recognition?

Can you name a godly person in Scripture who retired?

Do you think retirement, as it is currently practiced in our culture, is biblically permissible?

What is your view of retirement?

DAY SIX

PONDER YOUR FUTURE

Ephesians 2:10 reads, *"For we are His workmanship, created in Christ Jesus for good works, which God prepared beforehand, that we should walk in them."* Each of us has a specific call or vocation which the Lord intends for us. He has given us the talents, abilities and spiritual gifts to function well in the vocation He has for us. List your dominant talents and abilities. (You may want to seek the counsel of those close to you for their assessment.)

Do you have a passionate or deep level of excitement about a particular vocation? If so, describe it.

What steps have you taken to either identify your future vocation or to prepare for it?

Have you identified a potential mentor who is involved in the career you are interested in pursuing? If so, who is it? When will you ask them to share their experience with you?

If you have not identified a potential mentor, how will you attempt to do so?

REMAINING AGENDA _____ (10 minutes)

Review what the students are required to do for the next lesson:

- Complete the Debt Homework on pages 57 to 60 in the Student Manual.
- Memorize *Proverbs 22:7*.
- Complete the practical applications of Debt List and Debt Repayment Schedule.

For small groups, in addition to the Remaining Agenda above: _____ (15 minutes)

1. Note in the Prayer Logs requests and answers to prayers.
2. End in prayer.

CROWN'S OVERVIEW OF CHAPTER 5

Debt is a serious struggle for many and is consistently discouraged in Scripture. One of the primary objectives of this lesson should be to challenge the students to establish the goal of becoming or staying debt free.

Agenda

1. _____(5 minutes) Open in prayer.

2. _____(5 minutes) Have each person individually recite from memory:

> *"Just as the rich rule the poor, so the borrower is servant to the lender"* (Proverbs 22:7).

3. _____(5 minutes) Confirm that everyone has completed the practical applications of Debt List and Debt Repayment Schedule.

4. _____(80 minutes) Begin the small group discussion.

DAY ONE

Read Deuteronomy 15:4-6; Deuteronomy 28:1-2,12 and Deuteronomy 28:15,43-45. According to these passages, how was debt viewed in the Old Testament? How is it viewed today?

[In Scripture debt was considered a curse, while being free from debt (being a lender) was a blessing. Today you are encouraged by peer pressure and the media to go into debt — with no limits — to acquire whatever the advertising industry says you *must* have.]

What was the cause of someone getting in debt (becoming a borrower) or getting out of debt?

[Disobedience led to debt and obedience led to getting out of debt (becoming a lender).]

DAY TWO

Read Romans 13:8; Proverbs 22:7 and 1 Corinthians 7:23 and answer: Is debt encouraged in Scripture? Why?

Romans 13:8 — [We are encouraged to stay out of debt.]

Proverbs 22:7 — [The debtor is servant to the lender.]

1 Corinthians 7:23 — [We are instructed not to be slaves of men. Therefore, make every effort to get out and stay out of debt. To summarize: the Bible does not say that debt is sin, but it clearly discourages indebtedness.]

How does this apply to you?

Do you have a strategy to avoid debt? Do you have a plan to get out of debt? If so, please describe your strategies.

DAY THREE_____

Read Psalm 37:21 and Proverbs 3:27-28. What do these verses say about debt repayment and paying current bills?

Psalm 37:21 — [A person who borrows but does not repay debts is called "wicked."]

Proverbs 3:27 - 28 — [Pay debts promptly if you have the resources. Many are taught to delay repayment to use other people's money as long as possible, but this is not biblical.]

How does this differ from the practices of our culture?

 _____ *Small Group Leader, you should have approximately **one hour** of class time remaining. We recommend a three-minute stretch break for your group at this time.*

DAY FOUR

Read Proverbs 22:26-27 and Proverbs 17:18. What does the Bible say about cosigning (striking hands, surety)?

Proverbs 22:26-27 — [Do not cosign. You may lose assets you need if you cosign.]

Proverbs 17:18 — [It is poor judgment to cosign.]

Should parents cosign for their children? Why?

Then read Proverbs 6:1-5. If someone has cosigned, what should he or she attempt to do? [If we have cosigned, we are to humbly and diligently seek the release of our obligation.]

DAY FIVE

Read the Debt Notes and answer: What did you learn about debt that proved to be especially helpful?

Why do you think using credit cards can be dangerous for some people?

What will you do to protect yourself from misusing credit cards?

DAY SIX

PONDER YOUR FUTURE

You may purchase a home some day. Before reading about home mortgages on pages 69 to 70 did you understand how much interest you would be required to pay for the mortgage?

Describe how you could minimize the amount of interest you would pay.

REMAINING AGENDA _____ (10 minutes)

Review what the students are required to do for the next lesson:

- Complete the Honesty Homework on pages 73 to 77 in the Student Manual.

- Memorize *Leviticus 19:11* .

- Complete the practical application of Estimated Budget.

 For small groups, in addition to the Remaining Agenda above: _____ (15 minutes)

1. Note in the Prayer Logs requests and answers to prayer.

2. End in prayer.

Reminder for small group leaders: Encourage your students to continue to meditate on God's Word.

CROWN'S OVERVIEW OF CHAPTER 6

Dishonest practices are common, but the Lord demands that His children act with absolute honesty and integrity. This section is one of the most challenging of the entire study.

Agenda

1. _____(5 minutes) Open in prayer.

2. _____(5 minutes) Have each person individually recite from memory:

> *"You shall not steal, nor deal falsely, nor lie to one another"* (Leviticus 19:11).

3. _____(5 minutes) Confirm that everyone has completed the practical application of Estimated Budget.

4. _____(80 minutes) Begin the small group discussion.

DAY ONE

Read Leviticus 19:11-13; Deuteronomy 25:13-16; Ephesians 4:25 and 1 Peter 1:15-16. What do these verses communicate to you about God's demand for honesty?

Leviticus 19:11-13 — [The Lord commands us to be honest.]

Deuteronomy 25:13-16 — [The Lord demands honesty in our business dealings.]

Ephesians 4:25 — [We are not to lie to one another.]

1 Peter 1:15-16 — [We are to be holy in our behavior just as the Lord is holy.]

Are you consistently honest in even the smallest details? If not, how do you propose to change?

What are two factors that motivate or influence us to act dishonestly?

[Some of the factors influencing dishonesty: greed, fearing that God will not provide for us, financial difficulties and peer pressure.]

1.

2.

How does this apply to you?

DAY TWO_____

Read Proverbs 14:2 and answer: Can you practice dishonesty and still love God? Why?

[The Lord requires leaders to be honest. A major criterion for selecting leadership was honesty, because a leader will influence those under his authority either for good or evil.]

Then read Proverbs 26:28 and Romans 13:9-10. According to these passages, can you practice dishonesty and still love your neighbor? Why?

[No, because a dishonest person hates those whom he hurts. But love does no wrong to a neighbor.]

DAY THREE_____

Read Psalm 15:1-5; Proverbs 12:22; Proverbs 20:7 and Isaiah 33:15-16 and answer: What are some of the benefits of honesty?

Psalm 15:1-5 — [More intimate fellowship with the Lord.]

Proverbs 12:22 — [An honest person is a delight to the Lord.]

Proverbs 20:7 — [The children of the honest are blessed.]

Isaiah 33:15-16 — [The Lord will protect and provide for the needs of the honest.]

Then read Proverbs 3:32; Proverbs 13:11 and Proverbs 21:6. What are some of the curses of dishonesty?

Proverbs 3:32 — [A dishonest person is an abomination to the Lord.]

Proverbs 13:11 — [Anything obtained dishonestly will be taken away.]

Proverbs 21:6 — [Obtaining wealth by lying yields only temporary gains and eventually leads to death.]

 _____ *Small Group Leader, you should have approximately* **one hour** *of class time remaining. We recommend a three-minute stretch break for your group at this time.*

DAY FOUR_____

Read Exodus 22:1-4; Numbers 5:5-8 and Luke 19:8 and answer: What does the Bible say about restitution?

[Restitution was required under the Old Testament law, and Zaccheus is an example of a person fulfilling this obligation. Restitution involved the return of the item acquired dishonestly plus a penalty.]

If you have acquired anything dishonestly, how will you make restitution?

[Ask forgiveness from the Lord, confess your dishonesty to the one who was harmed and make full restitution. Sometimes restitution is a delicate and complex issue. The question of how to fulfill the principle of restitution should be prayerfully answered.]

DAY FIVE

Read the Honesty Notes and answer: How does the example of Abraham in *Genesis 14:21-23* challenge you to be honest?

[We should be honest in even the small details of life.]

Describe any ways you are tempted to be dishonest in small matters.

Then read Exodus 23:8; Proverbs 15:27 and Proverbs 29:4. What is the biblical position on bribes? Have you ever been asked to give or take a bribe? If so, describe what happened.

[You must never take a bribe, because it will influence your judgment. The person who is not involved with bribes will live, but a leader who takes bribes will be overthrown.]

DAY SIX

PONDER YOUR FUTURE

Read Exodus 18:21-22 and answer: Does the Lord require honesty for leaders? Why?

[The Lord requires leaders to be honest because a leader will influence those under his authority either for good or evil.]

Then read Proverbs 28:16 and Proverbs 29:12. What are the consequences of dishonesty for people in leadership?

Proverbs 28:16 — [A dishonest person will be removed from leadership.]

Proverbs 29:12 — [Subordinates will become dishonest.]

Have you ever had to interface with a dishonest leader? If so, how did you feel?

Are you currently in a position of leadership? If so, describe benefits you would experience as a leader for being totally honest.

Think of future leadership positions you aspire to hold (in parenting, in business, in education, in church or in ministry). Describe the character qualities that these positions require.

REMAINING AGENDA _____ (10 minutes)

Review what the students are required to do for the next lesson.

- Complete the Counsel Homework on pages 91 to 95 in the Student Manual.

- Memorize *Proverbs 12:15*.

- Complete the practical application of Adjusting Your Budget.

For small groups, in addition to the Remaining Agenda above: _____ (15 minutes)

1. Note in the Prayer Log requests and answers to prayers.

2. End in prayer.

CROWN'S OVERVIEW OF CHAPTER 7

Everyone should seek counsel when they need to make a major financial decision. Our culture consistently discourages people from seeking counsel.

Agenda

1. _____(5 minutes) Open in prayer.

2. _____(5 minutes) Have each person individually recite from memory:

> *"The way of a fool is right in his own eyes, but a wise man is he who listens to counsel"* (Proverbs 12:15).

3. _____(5 minutes) Confirm that everyone has completed the practical application of Adjusting Your Budget.

4. _____(80 minutes) Begin the group discussion.

DAY ONE

Read Proverbs 12:15; Proverbs 13:10 and Proverbs 15:22 and answer: What are some of the benefits of seeking counsel?

Proverbs 12:15 — [The person who listens to counsel is wise.]

Proverbs 13:10 — [Wisdom comes to those who seek counsel, but the consequence of not seeking counsel is strife.]

Proverbs 15:22 — [Plans succeed with counsel, but fail without it.]

What are some of the benefits you have experienced from seeking counsel?

What hinders you from seeking counsel?

DAY TWO_____

Read Psalm 16:7 and Psalm 32:8 and answer: Does the Lord actively counsel His children?

{Yes, the Lord actively counsels His children.]

Then read Psalm 106:13-15. In this passage what was the consequence of not seeking the Lord's counsel?

[A "wasting disease" was sent because they did not seek the counsel of the Lord.]

Have you ever suffered for not seeking the Lord's counsel? If so, describe what happened.

How do you personally seek the Lord's counsel?

[We seek the counsel of the Lord primarily through prayer, the Bible and godly people.]

DAY THREE_____

Read Psalm 119:24; Psalm 119:105; 2 Timothy 3:16-17 and Hebrews 4:12. Why should the Bible also serve as your counselor?

[We must seek the counsel of the Word of God because it is living, and it gives us direction for our lives.]

Then read Psalm 119:98-100. Living by the counsel of Scripture will:

[Make us wiser than our enemies, our teachers and those more experienced.]

Do you read and study the Bible as consistently as you should? If not, what prevents your consistency?

_____ *Small Group Leader, you should have approximately* **one hour** *of class time remaining. We recommend a three-minute stretch break for your group at this time.*

DAY FOUR

Read Proverbs 1:8-9. Who should be among your counselors?

[Our parents should be among our counselors.]

Do you actively seek counsel from your parents? If not, why?

Read Proverbs 11:14 and Ecclesiastes 4:9-12. What do these verses communicate to you?

Proverbs 11:14 — [People fail without counsel, but many counselors lead to victory.]

Ecclesiastes 4:9-12 — [Two or three people working together are more productive than a single individual.]

How do you propose to apply this principle?

Read Psalm 1:1-3 and answer: Whom should you avoid as a counselor?

[Avoid the wicked as your counselor.]

What is your definition of a wicked person?

[A wicked person is one who lives his life without regard to God.]

Is there ever a circumstance in which you should seek the input of a person who does not know Christ? If so, when?

DAY FIVE HOMEWORK

Read the Counsel Notes and answer: What in the notes particularly interested you?

What issues are you currently facing that require wise counsel?

Who will you ask for advice concerning these issues?

DAY SIX

PONDER YOUR FUTURE

Who do you think should be the number one counselor of a husband? Of a wife? Why?

[The husband and wife are are each other's most important counselors because they are one.]

REMAINING AGENDA _____(10 minutes)

Review what the students are required to do for the next lesson.

- Complete the Giving Homework on pages 107 to 111 in the Student Manual.
- Memorize *Acts 20:35* .
- Complete the practical application of Beginning Your Budget.

 For small groups, in addition to the Remaining Agenda above: _____ (15 minutes)

1. Note in the Prayer Logs requests and answers to prayer.
2. End in prayer.

 Reminder for Small Group Leaders: Remember to complete the students' evaluations. Also, be faithful to contact each student this week and note this in the Care Log.

CROWN'S OVERVIEW OF CHAPTER 8

Read the Giving Notes prior to attending the week 8 study. Concentrate on communicating to the students the importance of giving with the proper attitude.

Agenda:

1. _____(5 minutes) Open in prayer.

2. _____(5 minutes) Have every person individually recite from memory:

> *"Remember the words of the Lord Jesus, that He himself said. 'It is more blessed to give than to receive'"* (Acts 20:35).

3. _____(5 minutes) Confirm that everyone has completed the practical application of Beginning Your Budget.

4. _____(80 minutes) Begin the group discussion.

DAY ONE

Read 1 Corinthians 13:3 and 2 Corinthians 9:7 and answer: What do these passages communicate about the importance of the proper attitude in giving?

1 Corinthians 13:3 — [Giving without a heart of love is of no value to the giver.]

2 Corinthians 9:7 — [Do not give grudgingly or under compulsion, but rather cheerfully. The proper attitude is crucial.]

How do you think a person can develop the proper attitude in giving?

[The proper attitude is *the key issue* in the area of giving. The only way to give out of a heart of love is to consciously give each gift to Jesus Christ Himself as an act of worship.]

After prayerfully evaluating your attitude in giving, how would you describe it?

DAY TWO_____

Read Acts 20:35 and answer: How does this principle from God's economy differ from the way most people view giving?

[In the Lord's economic system it is more blessed to give than to receive. Man's economic system operates under the reverse assumption.]

List the benefits for the giver, which are found in each of the following passages:

Proverbs 11:24-25 — [There is a material increase — in the Lord's time and way — to the giver.]

Matthew 6:20 — [We can lay up treasures in heaven which we will be able to enjoy throughout all eternity.]

Luke 12:34 — [The heart of the giver is drawn to Christ as treasures are given to Him.]

1 Timothy 6:18-19 — [We can store treasures in heaven and *"take hold of that which is life indeed."*]

DAY THREE_____

Read Malachi 3:8-10. Was the tithe required under Old Testament Law?

[The tithe was required under the Law, and it was considered robbing God not to give these required gifts.]

Then read 2 Corinthians 8:1-5. Identify three principles from this passage that should influence how much you give.

1. [They first gave themselves to the Lord asking Him to direct their giving. In the same way we need to submit ourselves to the Lord when determining how much to give.]

2. [They were so yielded to the Lord that despite difficult circumstances they begged to give.]

3. [They experienced tremendous joy as a result of their sacrificial giving.]

Prayerfully seek the Lord's guidance to determine how much you should give. You will not be asked to disclose the amount.

Read 1 Timothy 5:8 and answer: Does the Bible require us to take care of our family members?

[Yes, we are required to take care of family members.]

How does this apply to you?

Then read Galatians 6:6 and 1 Timothy 5:17-18. What do these verses tell you about financially supporting your church and those who teach the Scriptures?

Galatians 6:6 — [Those who are taught the Scriptures should financially support their teachers.]

1 Timothy 5:17-18 —[God's New Testament instrument is the local church, and we are to adequately support those who serve as pastors and teachers.]

_____ *Small Group Leader, you should have approximately* **one hour** *of class time remaining. We recommend a three-minute stretch break for your group at this time.*

DAY FOUR

Read Isaiah 58:6-11 and Ezekiel 16:49 and answer: What do these verses say about giving to the poor?

Isaiah 58:6-11 — [When we give to the poor, the Lord will protect us, answer our prayers and bless us with His joy.]

Ezekiel 16:49 — [The primary sins of Sodom were pride and not caring for the poor — even though they had an abundance of material goods.]

Then study Matthew 25:35-45. How does Jesus Christ identify with the poor?

[Jesus identifies personally with the poor. When we give to the poor we are giving to Christ Himself. When we do not give to the poor, we are not giving to Christ, and He is left hungry and naked.]

Then read Galatians 2:9-10. What does this verse communicate to you about giving to the poor?

[Giving to the poor was a very high priority among the apostles.]

Are you currently giving to the poor? If not, what is hindering you?

DAY FIVE

Read the Giving Notes and answer: How will your recognition of the importance of giving with the proper attitude impact your giving?

What did you learn about giving that proved especially interesting? In what way?

DAY SIX

PONDER YOUR FUTURE

Write your "autobiography of giving" by describing your attitude toward giving, how much you have given and who you have given to:

Now take time and pray. Ask the Lord to give you His vision for your future giving. Describe your sense of what the Lord wants your giving to be in the future.

REMAINING AGENDA _____ (10 minutes)

Review what the students are required to do for the next lesson.

- Complete the Saving Homework on pages 125 to 130 in the Student Manual.
- Memorize *Proverbs 21:20* and *Proverbs 21:5* .
- Review the practical application of Insurance and Standard of Living.

 For small groups, in addition to the Remaining Agenda above: _____ (15 minutes)

1. Note in the Prayer Log requests and answers to prayers.
2. End in prayer.

CROWN'S OVERVIEW OF CHAPTER 9

This chapter's objectives are to make the students aware of the proper biblical attitudes toward saving and investing and to educate them as to the scriptural framework for savings and investing. **The leaders should not recommend any specific investments or financial products or services. Crown Ministries assumes no liability for any actions taken related to specific investments or savings.**

Agenda:

1. _____(5 minutes) Open in prayer on your knees.

2. _____(5 minutes) Have everyone recite from memory:

> *"The wise man saves for the future, but the foolish man spends whatever he gets"* (Proverbs 21:20,LB).
> *"Steady plodding brings prosperity; hasty speculation brings poverty"* (Proverbs 21:5,LB).

3. _____(5 minutes) Confirm that everyone has completed the practical application of Insurance and Standard of Living.

4. _____(10 minutes) Ask the students to share their creative ideas on how to save money each week that would normally be spent.

5. _____(70 minutes) Begin the group discussion.

DAY ONE

Read Genesis 41:34-36; Proverbs 21:20 and Proverbs 30:24-25 and answer: What do these passages communicate to you about savings?

Genesis 41:34-36 — [Joseph saved during a time of plenty to prepare for a coming famine.]

Proverbs 21:20 — [Those who are wise save, but the foolish only consume.]

Proverbs 30:24-25 — [Ants are commended as wise because they save.]

Read Luke 12:16-21, 34. Why did the Lord call the rich man a fool?

[The rich man was a fool because he stored up all his goods (v. 18) and was not rich toward God.]

According to this parable, why do you think it is scripturally permissible to save only when you are also giving?

[If we save without giving, our hearts will be drawn to those possessions and away from Christ (v. 34).]

DAY TWO_____

Read 1 Timothy 5:8 and answer: What is a scripturally acceptable goal for saving?

[It is permissible to save to meet the needs of our family.]

Then read 1 Timothy 6:9. What is a scripturally unacceptable reason for saving?

[It is wrong to desire to get rich. However, it is not wrong to become rich if it is a by-product of being a faithful steward.]

Then read 1 Timothy 6:10. According to this verse, why is it wrong to want to get rich (refer to *1 Timothy 6:9*)?

[When we want to get rich we are actually loving money. The desire to get rich is common in our culture, and this attitude can destroy our fellowship with the Lord.]

Do you have the desire to get rich?

Then read 1 Timothy 6:11. What should you do if you have the desire to get rich?

[You should flee from this desire and pursue godly living.]

DAY THREE

Read Proverbs 21:5; Proverbs 24:27; Proverbs 27:23-24; Ecclesiastes 3:1; Ecclesiastes 11:2 and Isaiah 48:17-18. What investment principle can you glean from each of these verses, and how will you apply each principle to your life?

Proverbs 21:5 — [Be a diligent, steady plodder and not hasty in saving and investing.]

Proverbs 24:27 — [Build your means of producing an income before securing a house.]

Proverbs 27:23-24 — [Know the status of your assets at all times.]

Ecclesiastes 3:1 — [Timing is important in investing.]

Ecclesiastes 11:2 — [You should diversify your investments.]

Isaiah 48:17-18 — [The Lord is the One who teaches us to prosper, and we need to seek Him as we make investment decisions.]

 _____*Small Group Leader, you should have approximately* **one hour** *of class time remaining. We recommend a three-minute stretch break for your group at this time.*

DAY FOUR

Gambling is defined as playing games of chance for money, betting, taking great risks and speculating. Some of today's most common forms of gambling are casino wagering, betting on sporting events, horse races, gambling over the Internet and state-run lotteries. What are some of the motivations that cause people to gamble?

[People are motivated to gamble by the desire to get rich quick, greed, and by the prospect of getting something for nothing. Many want to become wealthy so they can quit working.]

Do these motives please the Lord? Why?

[These motives do not please the Lord because they are completely contrary to His principles found in the Bible.]

Read Proverbs 28:20 and Proverbs 28:22. According to these passages, why do you think a godly person should not gamble (play lotteries, bet on sporting events, etc.)?

[A person who hastens after wealth is identified as evil and will experience poverty. Please encourage your students never to bet one penny. State lotteries are particularly enticing because they have been legalized by the government and glamorized by the media.]

How does gambling contradict the scriptural principles of working diligently and being a faithful steward of the Lord's possessions?

[Gambling is in direct opposition to the scriptural principles of diligent work and faithful stewardship. No productive work is required in gambling, thus a person's character is not properly developed. The odds of winning are absurdly low, and a gambler is really wasting the possessions the Lord has entrusted to him. A tide of gambling has swept our nation. There are about five million compulsive gamblers (more than one million of whom are teens). Gambling among college students is rising rapidly.]

DAY FIVE

Read the Saving Notes and answer: What was the most important information in the notes?

How will you apply this to your life?

DAY SIX_____

PONDER YOUR FUTURE

Carefully study the principle of compounding on page 134. Assume you saved about $20 each week (about $1,000 per year) and earned ten percent. How much would you accumulate by age 65 if you started this saving plan today?

$ _____ (Refer to the graph on page 135.)

Describe the specific steps you intend to take to begin saving.

REMAINING AGENDA _____(10 minutes)

Review what the students are required to do for the next lesson.

- Complete Your Future Homework on pages 143 to 147 in the student manual.

- Memorize Philippians 4:11-13.

- Explain the practical application of Checking Account and Budget Summary.

For small groups, in addition to the Remaining Agenda above: _____ (15 minutes)

1. Note in the Prayer Log requests and answers to prayers.

2. End in prayer.

CROWN'S OVERVIEW OF CHAPTER 10

This week we will concentrate on determining our God-given standard of living. In many respects this section is the summary of the entire study.

Agenda:

1. _____(5 minutes) Open in prayer.

2. _____(5 minutes) Have everyone individually recite from memory:

> *"For I have learned to be content in whatever circumstances I am. I know how to get along with humble means, and I also know how to live in prosperity; in any and every circumstance I have learned the secret of being filled and going hungry, both of having abundance and suffering need. I can do all things through Him who strengthens me"* (Philippians 4:11-13).

3. _____(5 minutes) Confirm that everyone has completed the practical application of Checking Account and Budget Summary and is budgeting faithfully. Discuss with the students the importance of a will.

4. _____(80 minutes) Begin the group discussion.

DAY ONE

When you begin your career, you will be faced with paying a variety of taxes.

Read Matthew 22:17-21 and Romans 13:1-7 and answer: Does the Lord require us to pay taxes to the government? Why?

[The Lord requires us to pay taxes because He instituted government to serve people. The consequence of tax evasion is punishment.]

Do you think it is biblically permissible to reduce your taxes by using legal tax deductions or shelters? Why?

[The government authorizes the use of legal tax deductions, but we should be careful not to make unwise investments simply to reduce taxes.]

DAY TWO_____

If you marry, you may become a parent.

Read Deuteronomy 6:6-7; Deuteronomy 11:18-19; Proverbs 22:6 and Ephesians 6:4.
According to these passages, who is responsible for teaching children how to handle money from a biblical perspective?

[It is the parents' responsibility to train their children to handle money.]

Stop and reflect for a few minutes. Describe how well you were prepared to manage money when you left home to attend college.

DAY THREE_____

Read Luke 3:14; Philippians 4:11-13; 1 Timothy 6:6-8 and Hebrews 13:5-6. What do each of these passages communicate to you about contentment?

Luke 3:14 — [Be content with your wages.]

Philippians 4:11-13 — [Contentment is not something that occurs naturally. It is learned. We can learn to be content in any circumstance.]

1 Timothy 6:6-8 — [Godliness with contentment is a means of great gain. We cannot take anything with us when we die, and we should be content with our basic needs satisfied.]

Hebrews 13:5-6 — [Because the Lord is our Protector and Provider. We are admonished not to love money and to be content with what we have.]

In our culture, why is it so difficult to be content?

How do you propose to practice contentment?

 _____*Small Group Leader, you should have approximately* **one hour** *of class time remaining. We recommend a three-minute stretch break for your group at this time.*

DAY FOUR

Read Hebrews 11:24-26. What does this passage tell you about making choices with an eternal perspective?

[Moses was a godly person who decided to live for eternal values rather than for the temporary treasures of this life.]

How will this impact you?

Then read Mark 8:36-37; Acts 4:32-37; 2 Corinthians 8:13-15 and 1 Thessalonians 4:11-12. What do these passages communicate to you about lifestyle?

Mark 8:36-37 — [A person can become tremendously wealthy, but without Christ it is meaningless.]

Acts 4:32-37 — [An equality of needs being met within the body of Christ led to revival.]

2 Corinthians 8:13-15 — [All basic needs should be met within the Christian community.]

1 Thessalonians 4:11-12 — [We are encouraged to live a quiet, industrious life.]

List three lifestyle changes you have made since beginning the study:

DAY FIVE

Read the Your Future Notes and answer: What in the notes proved especially challenging or helpful?

What has been the most beneficial part of the study for you? Why?

Reflect on your time during the study. Describe several insights you have gained from others in your class that proved especially encouraging.

DAY SIX

PONDER YOUR FUTURE

What will you commit to implement from the study during the next month?

What will you commit to implement from the study during the next three months?

Who will hold you accountable for accomplishing these commitments?

REMAINING AGENDA _____ (10 minutes)

Instruct your students to complete the Evaluation and Suggestion sheet found in the Practical Application Workbook. The input from the students is very important for the continued improvement of this study. The students' Evaluation and Suggestion sheet should be turned in to the leader before the end of the study and then forwarded to Crown Ministries, 530 Crown Oak Centre Drive, Longwood, Florida 32750.

1. Note in the Prayer Logs requests and answers to prayers.

2. End in prayer.

TEACHER'S EVALUATION AND SUGGESTIONS

Crown Ministries wants to obtain your counsel. The suggestions and insights of past participants have significantly improved the study. Please forward this along with your students' evaluations to either your church or directly to Crown Ministries. **Please print clearly.** Thank you!

Name: | | | | | | | | | | | | | | | | | | | | | | | | | | | | | | | | | | | Date: | | | |

Address: | | | | | | | | | | | | | | | | | | | | | | | | | | | | | | | | | | | | | | | |

City: | | | | | | | | | | | | | | | | | | | | | | | State: | | | Zip: | | | | | |—| | | | |

Phone No: | | | |—| | | |—| | | | | College or Church Affiliation: | | | | | | | | | | | | | | | | | | |

1. What was the most valuable part of the study? Please be specific.

2. Do you have any suggestions on improving any areas?

3. Describe any insights that would help others:

4. We would be appreciative if you would share on the back of this page what the Lord has done in your life through this study or any practical hints that would be especially helpful.

What the Crown Ministries study has meant to me:

Practical Hints:

EVALUATION OF STUDENTS

It is important to track the performance of your students to determine who is faithful. Place your students' names where indicated and place an "x" each week in the appropriate box when they have been faithful in their attendance, scripture memory, practical application or homework. Leave a box blank if they are not faithful in that particular area.

WEEK	Student Name ➤ REQUIREMENTS								WEEK							
1	ATTENDANCE								**6**							
	SCRIPTURE MEMORY															
	PRACTICAL APPLICATION															
	HOMEWORK															
2	ATTENDANCE								**7**							
	SCRIPTURE MEMORY															
	PRACTICAL APPLICATION															
	HOMEWORK															
3	ATTENDANCE								**8**							
	SCRIPTURE MEMORY															
	PRACTICAL APPLICATION															
	HOMEWORK															
4	ATTENDANCE								**9**							
	SCRIPTURE MEMORY															
	PRACTICAL APPLICATION															
	HOMEWORK															
5	ATTENDANCE								**10**							
	SCRIPTURE MEMORY															
	PRACTICAL APPLICATION															
	HOMEWORK															

CARE LOG

Leaders: _____

Beginning Date of Small Group Study: _____

	Initials of Leader responsible for contact	S T U D E N T S							
WEEK 1									
2									
3									
4									
5									
6									
7									
8									
9									
10									

DESCRIPTION OF FIRST SOCIAL ACTIVITY (WEEK FIVE): _____

_____

DESCRIPTION OF SECOND SOCIAL ACTIVITY (WEEK TEN): _____

_____

PRAYER LOG

Name: _____

Phone: _____

Address: _____

_____

E-Mail Address: _____

Week	Prayer Request(s)	Answers to Prayer
1		
2		
3		
4		
5		
6		
7		
8		
9		
10	My long-term prayer request:	

"Pray for one another ..." **(James 5:16).**

PRAYER LOG

Name: _____

Phone: _____

Address: _____

_____

E-Mail Address: _____

Week	Prayer Request(s)	Answers to Prayer
1		
2		
3		
4		
5		
6		
7		
8		
9		
10	My long-term prayer request:	

"Pray for one another ..." **(James 5:16).**

P R A Y E R   L O G

Name: _____

Phone: _____

Address: _____

_____

E-Mail Address: _____

Week	Prayer Request(s)	Answers to Prayer
1		
2		
3		
4		
5		
6		
7		
8		
9		
10	My long-term prayer request:	

"Pray for one another ..." **(James 5:16).**

PRAYER LOG

Name: _____

Phone: _____

Address: _____

_____

E-Mail Address: _____

Week	Prayer Request(s)	Answers to Prayer
1		
2		
3		
4		
5		
6		
7		
8		
9		
10	My long-term prayer request:	

"Pray for one another ..." **(James 5:16).**

PRAYER LOG

Name: _____

Phone: _____

Address: _____

_____

E-Mail Address: _____

Week	Prayer Request(s)	Answers to Prayer
1		
2		
3		
4		
5		
6		
7		
8		
9		
10	My long-term prayer request:	

"Pray for one another ..." **(James 5:16).**

P R A Y E R L O G

Name: _____

Phone: _____

Address: _____

_____

E-Mail Address: _____

Week	Prayer Request(s)	Answers to Prayer
1		
2		
3		
4		
5		
6		
7		
8		
9		
10	My long-term prayer request:	

"Pray for one another ..." **(James 5:16).**

PRAYER LOG

Name: _____

Phone: _____

Address: _____

_____

E-Mail Address: _____

Week	Prayer Request(s)	Answers to Prayer
1		
2		
3		
4		
5		
6		
7		
8		
9		
10	My long-term prayer request:	

"Pray for one another ..." **(James 5:16).**

P R A Y E R   L O G

Name: _____

Phone: _____

Address: _____

_____

E-Mail Address: _____

Week	Prayer Request(s)	Answers to Prayer
1		
2		
3		
4		
5		
6		
7		
8		
9		
10	My long-term prayer request:	

"Pray for one another ..." **(James 5:16).**

Crown Ministries wants to obtain your counsel. The suggestions and insights of past participants have significantly improved the study. Please forward this along with your students' evaluations to either your church or directly to Crown Ministries. **Please print clearly.** Thank you!

Name: |⎵|⎵|⎵|⎵|⎵|⎵|⎵|⎵|⎵|⎵|⎵|⎵|⎵|⎵|⎵|⎵|⎵|⎵|⎵|⎵|⎵|⎵|⎵|⎵|⎵|⎵|⎵|⎵|⎵| Date: |⎵|⎵|⎵|

Address: |⎵|⎵|⎵|⎵|⎵|⎵|⎵|⎵|⎵|⎵|⎵|⎵|⎵|⎵|⎵|⎵|⎵|⎵|⎵|⎵|⎵|⎵|⎵|⎵|⎵|⎵|⎵|⎵|⎵|⎵|⎵|⎵|⎵|⎵|⎵|

City: |⎵|⎵|⎵|⎵|⎵|⎵|⎵|⎵|⎵|⎵|⎵|⎵|⎵|⎵|⎵|⎵|⎵|⎵|⎵| State: |⎵|⎵| Zip: |⎵|⎵|⎵|⎵|⎵|–|⎵|⎵|⎵|⎵|

Phone No: |⎵|⎵|⎵|–|⎵|⎵|⎵|–|⎵|⎵|⎵|⎵| College or Church Affiliation: |⎵|⎵|⎵|⎵|⎵|⎵|⎵|⎵|⎵|⎵|⎵|⎵|⎵|⎵|⎵|⎵|⎵|

1. What was the most valuable part of the study? Please be specific.

2. Do you have any suggestions on improving any areas?

3. Describe any insights that would help others:

4. We would be appreciative if you would share on the back of this page what the Lord has done in your life through this study or any practical hints that would be especially helpful.

What the Crown Ministries study has meant to me:

Practical Hints:

It is important to track the performance of your students to determine who is faithful. Place your students' names where indicated and place an "x" each week in the appropriate box when they have been faithful in their attendance, scripture memory, practical application or homework. Leave a box blank if they are not faithful in that particular area.

WEEK	Student Name ➤ REQUIREMENTS						WEEK					
1	ATTENDANCE						**6**					
	SCRIPTURE MEMORY											
	PRACTICAL APPLICATION											
	HOMEWORK											
2	ATTENDANCE						**7**					
	SCRIPTURE MEMORY											
	PRACTICAL APPLICATION											
	HOMEWORK											
3	ATTENDANCE						**8**					
	SCRIPTURE MEMORY											
	PRACTICAL APPLICATION											
	HOMEWORK											
4	ATTENDANCE						**9**					
	SCRIPTURE MEMORY											
	PRACTICAL APPLICATION											
	HOMEWORK											
5	ATTENDANCE						**10**					
	SCRIPTURE MEMORY											
	PRACTICAL APPLICATION											
	HOMEWORK											

Leaders: _____

Beginning Date of Small Group Study: _____

	Initials of Leader responsible for contact	S T U D E N T S							
WEEK 1									
2									
3									
4									
5									
6									
7									
8									
9									
10									

DESCRIPTION OF FIRST SOCIAL ACTIVITY (WEEK FIVE): _____

_____

DESCRIPTION OF SECOND SOCIAL ACTIVITY (WEEK TEN): _____

_____

PRAYER LOG

Name: _____

Phone: _____

Address: _____

_____

E-Mail Address: _____

Week	Prayer Request(s)	Answers to Prayer
1		
2		
3		
4		
5		
6		
7		
8		
9		
10	My long-term prayer request:	

"Pray for one another ..." **(James 5:16).**

PRAYER LOG

Name: _____

Phone: _____

Address: _____

_____

E-Mail Address: _____

Week	Prayer Request(s)	Answers to Prayer
1		
2		
3		
4		
5		
6		
7		
8		
9		
10	My long-term prayer request:	

"Pray for one another ..." **(James 5:16).**

PRAYER LOG

Name: _____

Phone: _____

Address: _____

_____

E-Mail Address: _____

Week	Prayer Request(s)	Answers to Prayer
1		
2		
3		
4		
5		
6		
7		
8		
9		
10	My long-term prayer request:	

"Pray for one another ..." **(James 5:16).**

PRAYER LOG

Name: _____

Phone: _____

Address: _____

_____

E-Mail Address: _____

Week	Prayer Request(s)	Answers to Prayer
1		
2		
3		
4		
5		
6		
7		
8		
9		
10	My long-term prayer request:	

"Pray for one another ..." **(James 5:16).**

PRAYER LOG

Name: _____

Phone: _____

Address: _____

_____

E-Mail Address: _____

Week	Prayer Request(s)	Answers to Prayer
1		
2		
3		
4		
5		
6		
7		
8		
9		
10	My long-term prayer request:	

"Pray for one another ..." **(James 5:16).**

PRAYER LOG

Name: _____

Phone: _____

Address: _____

_____

E-Mail Address: _____

Week	Prayer Request(s)	Answers to Prayer
1		
2		
3		
4		
5		
6		
7		
8		
9		
10	My long-term prayer request:	

"Pray for one another ..." **(James 5:16).**